# From Grandmas' Mouths to Babes

Millicent Simmons

ISBN 978-1-956001-39-6 (paperback)
ISBN 978-1-956001-40-2 (eBook)

Copyright © 2021 by Millicent Simmons

All rights reserved. No part of this publication may be reproduced, distributed, or transmitted in any form or by any means, including photocopying, recording, or other electronic or mechanical methods without the prior written permission of the publisher.

Printed in the United States of America

# Dedication

This children's book is being dedicated to 3 special children in the life of the author. While the names have been changed and particular circumstances are fictitious, this author is thankful to the children who have inspired this writing. Be sure to expect other writings from this author based on the inspirational lives of the children of the world.

Once upon a time there were two little children, named Johnny and Bonnie, who were so excited about seeing their new, little sister. They were always playing, talking. and having fun together. They had heard about little sister but kept waiting, waiting, and waiting, as well as watching, to see her.

Finally, little sister was born, and her name was Anita. Although Anita was born, she was not talking and playing as they expected. They started playing with her and talking. Most of the time, they found little Anita just sleeping. They could be seen pulling her arm, and saying, "Hey, Anita", as they tried to get her to talk with them.

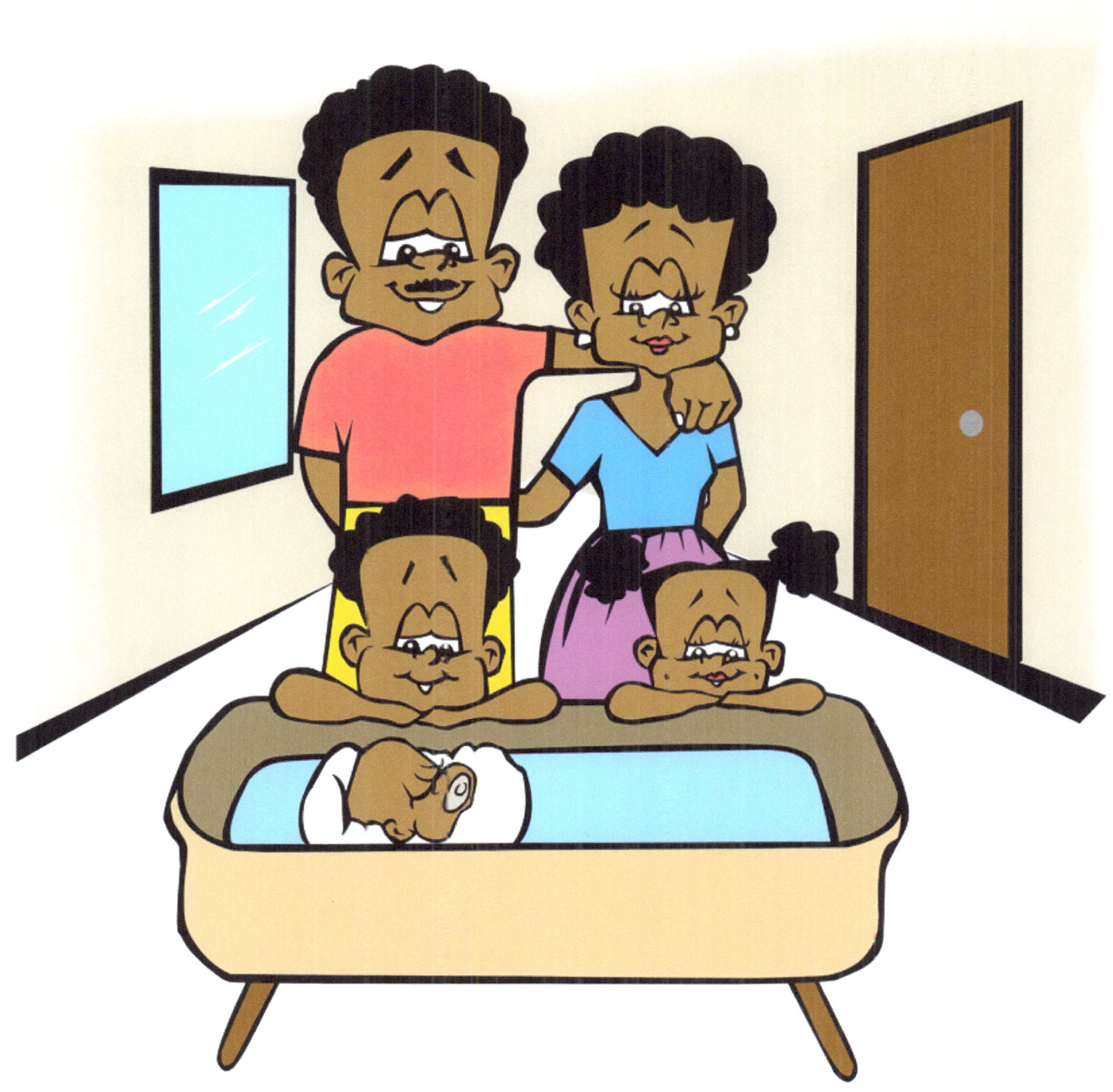

Well, grandma and grandpa's house was very, very close by and Johnny and Bonnie would visit daily. But when Anita came along, they wanted Anita to go with them to Grandma and grandpa's house. I could hear their mouths say, "I want to go see Anita." After they got where Anita was, she still was not talking to them. They tried to make her talk, but little Anita was just sleeping. Grandma explained to Johnny and Bonnie that Anita was acting like all other babies when they were newborns. Grandma told them that they should always let mom and dad know when little Anita was crying. However, sometimes mom and dad would think, *"Is Anita crying because she needs something or just because Johnny and Bonnie were doing something to her."* The big sister and brother always wanted to be near little Anita.

They would always follow grandma's instructions to help mom and dad with Anita: like putting her pacifier in her mouth, holding her hand, or getting something for mom/dad to have some kind of contact.

Johnny and Bonnie had another grandmother, whom they called Nana. They would travel to visit Nana and would spend the day or weekend with her. They loved Nana and Nana was always glad to see them. Nana would talk with them through FaceTime and this grandma would give them instructions similar to the other grandma. And they would exclaim, "Oh boy! Grandmas know about a lot of things." This information made them very happy.

Johnny and Bonnie continued to play together. You could hear Johnny say, "Bonnie, come play with me." Or, you could hear Bonnie say, "Johnny, come play with me." Johnny had drums and Bonnie had the kitchenette. They would play for a while and visit Anita for a while. There were times, Johnny would be playing the drums and wanted Bonnie to sing along with him and as his buddy, she did just that. When grandma would visit and go into Johnny's room, he would motion for her to sit down and sing along with him. Bonnie was small; but, she was always trying to do what her brother said.

Little Anita would be seen calmly sleeping and Johnny and Bonnie wanted her to say some words. Little Anita would at times sit and look around in the room, but still was not saying a word. The only thing they heard her say or do was "cry." They always wanted to help.

When daddy would get up and get his coat, Johnny and Bonnie would be ready also.

This meant they were going to see grandma. As you know, words were often from grandma's mouth and then "straight out of the mouths of babes."

Little Anita is opening her eyes more and oh boy!, she is getting all kinds of hugs and kisses. Johnny and Bonnie are full of excitement each day for Anita. They cannot wait to get home from school to give her lots of hugs/kisses. Anita is moving her arms more and opening her eyes for longer periods of time. Anita is making some noise with her mouth. Johnny and Bonnie are still talking and trying to play with her.

Johnny and Bonnie are always playing together and hoping for the day that little

Anita will be able to join them. Finally, just as grandma had promised, the day arrived, Anita could play along with them and they were happy thereafter.

# HADAR
## AND THE
## NEW STORY
### BOOK 1

## M.E. MURPHY

### Illustrated by Johanna Murphy

The content is the sole opinion and expression of the author, and not necessarily that of the publisher.

Copyright 2021 by M.E. Murphy.

All rights reserved. No part of this book may be reproduced, transmitted, or distributed in any form by any means, including, but not limited to, recording, photocopying, or taking screenshots of parts of the book, without prior written permission from the author or the publisher. Brief quotations for noncommercial purposes, such as book reviews, permitted by Fair Use of the U.S. Copyright Law, are allowed without written permissions, as long as such quotations do not cause damage to the book's commercial value.For permissions, write to the publisher, whose addressis stated below.

Printed in the United States of America.

ISBN 978-1-953150-88-2 (Paperback)
ISBN 978-1-953150-89-9 (Digital)

Lettra Press books maybe ordered through booksellers or by contacting:

Lettra Press LLC
30 N Gould St.Suite 4753
Sheridan, WY 82801
1 307-200-3414 | info@lettrapress.com
www.lettrapress.com

It's all a question of story. We are in trouble just now because we do not have a good story. We are in between stories. The Old Story—the account of how the world came to be and how we fit into it—is not functioning properly, and we have not learned the New Story.

—Thomas Berry

FOR

**Margaret**

# CHAPTER ONE
# THE BORDER

When the early spring nights seldom reach freezing, a man who was dressed comfortably walked the mountain road toward the border of a warring country. Standing with a simple walking stick, he stood face-to-face with a soldier guard. The soldier felt no threat and asked for his name and papers. The man only had a name: Hadar.

An unusual name, thought the guard as he lowered his weapon and escorted the man through the checkpoint.

The soldier signaled his comrades and waited, feeling at ease and thinking that the man looked familiar, yet he was sure they'd never met. Being the experienced soldier, he informed the others that he would accompany Hadar to the next station house. They mounted a jeep and left.

As they drove, the soldier began to talk about his worries, his emptiness, and his fears. He worried about his young wife and his neighbors that lived here in the warring country, the emptiness caused by their absence, and the fear that he might not return home to see them.

"Hadar, I am not a very spiritual man, yet I find myself often praying for peace."

"I too am a prayer for peace."

The soldier found these words meaningful yet mysterious as he answered,

"Amen."

## CHAPTER TWO
# THE STATION HOUSE

At the station house, the man was introduced as Mr. Hadar. "Please call me Hadar," he replied. The officer here was older and more cautious, yet he soon felt at ease and seemed happy to hear Hadar explain that he had come to help the country.

A few workers from the town were about and found the new arrival somewhat familiar and engaging. Inquiring as to his hometown, he assured them that it was close by. There seemed to be a place in his thoughts for everyone who caught his gaze or spoke to him. The perimeter about him was exciting to the heart.

As the senior soldier questioned Hadar, he learned that he came to bring peace. As they exchanged conversation, he began to feel a deepening respect, but his reason told him the stranger had much to learn about the big problems created by the holy wars in his country. This was warring for God and nothing less.

"Well, since you come from the border to wage peace,"—he smiled—"and are unarmed, I will take you to our headquarters in the town below. We as soldiers are also here for peace."

The winding road and the rapid speed caused Hadar to comment at how such a beautiful journey was passing so quickly. As the officer tried to explain the conflict and its source, Hadar sat and listened carefully as the soldier spoke:

"Religions here all have separate traditions, and the leaders have no way of agreeing because of their different beliefs. Therefore no one feels the wars can end. One group is always fighting the other or even between themselves. It has become a sad affair."

Hadar spoke, "Are not a person's beliefs much like a fingerprint?' The officer answered with a quiet nod as he pondered these odd words.

As they continued the journey, the soldier thought and dared to hope for peace. Just before arriving to the town, he turned to Hadar and said, "To wage peace, you will have to meet the town leader and continue on to the assembly at the capital. Our hope is with you."

# CHAPTER THREE
# THE TOWN

Word travelled faster than the jeep. The townspeople now knew that a man of peace was coming from the border. They were excited and knew that if the soldiers were escorting him, that he must be important and came with authority.

Excited people filled the main street of the town to see the stranger. The driver was surprised to hear people clapping and even more surprised that cheers erupted as they passed. Looking in his rearview mirror, he was amazed. He saw the small buds of the early spring plants and trees bursting into bloom as they passed.

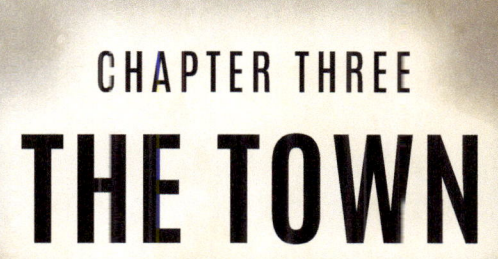

Hadar was greeted by the town leader at his home and invited to come and share a meal while they talked. The town leader was polite and reserved as they began to share his food. When they raised their cups in ritual courtesy, the gaze of Hadar was difficult to leave, and now the town leader felt the need to share.

As Hadar began to eat, the town leader spoke, "The soldiers have told me that you have come to wage peace. As a youth, I entered public service in the hope of seeing peace in my time. I was perhaps too young and too naïve while just finishing my second decade of life.

"The people are again excited by the chance of peace. It is again a new generation. I have seen it more than once come and go. As a young man, I was part of it. Yet now I see as people age, they replace their hopes with beliefs, and tension begins and conflicts return."

"The people are again excited by the chance of peace. It is again a new generation. I have seen it more than once come and go. As a young man, I was part of it. Yet now I see as people age, they replace their hopes with beliefs, and tension begins and conflicts return."

Upon leaving, the town leader returned his attention to Hadar and said, "I hear you have brought a miracle."

"Not I." Hadar smiled. "It was the earth answering the new hope and joy of your people."

Finishing their meal in a comfortable silence, the town leader seemed to find new flavor in these common late-winter foods.

As Hadar was departing from his home and their hands met, the town leader felt the need to exchange an embrace of friendship and hoped as he asked, "Do you have any words of advice for me?"

"Yes! It is spring, replant your hopes." As Hadar walked to the jeep for his journey to the capital, a young person asked, "Can you bring us peace?"

"I can bring what is needed, yet you must decide to need what I bring." With that, Hadar mounted another jeep and was off to the capital.

## CHAPTER FOUR
# THE CAPITAL

The capital was quiet in the early morning when they arrived. The soldiers were diligently saluting the car as it passed through checkpoints. In this busy urban surrounding, people were used to the arrival and departure of negotiators and representatives. Yet the excitement of the rural townspeople had reached the capital, and the authorities were anxious to have Hadar arrive early before people could gather.

As Hadar entered the capital building, the sunlight found its way through the early clouds and warmed the façade of the building's entrance. Hadar paused and took comfort and warmth in the morning light, the light of the earth's star! It appeared that the light delivered a message that strengthened Hadar's resolve.

Once through the door, he was escorted to the large negotiation room where the kingdom's religious leaders with their many aids sat in comfort, seriously exchanging ideas.

Hadar understood that he had arrived to the center of the war, a center much like the eye of a hurricane.

Hadar was introduced and was invited to take a seat. He sat in silence and heard his first question: "By what authority do you come?"

"My authority comes from the need of the people. As a man of the people, I carry a request for peace."

"We all believe in peace," said the priestess with some defiance, "yet our religions divide us."

"You're all united in the here and now, why are you divided about the unknown?"

When there was no response, Hadar continued, "Remember our earliest religions that we now find quaint. You no longer worship the wind or the clouds and find the gods of war and love storylike. Now, is your time to grow!"

There was silence, and then a question sounded loudly.

"What of God's words and the revelations of our prophets?" asked the priestess.

"What of the thousands of years of revelations since then?" Hadar countered with a quiet commanding strength and then continued, "You are the new prophets! Your men of science offer revelations, your men of literature and philosophy have holy insight. They too need to be in this room."

"What of our religious ways?" interrupted the majority leader.

"They were a beginning, and as many roads lead in the same direction, now is the time to join in the journey. Widen your paths!"

"How?"

Everyone felt Hadar's eyes reach inside them as his words challenged their lives:

"Write the new story!"

The priestess with disbelief and emotion said, "How can this be done?"

With pause and authority, Hadar answered, "Allow your beliefs to match your greatest hopes and wisdom, and not your worse fears and intolerances. Include your hearts and now your science in understanding who you are."

"How can we change the beliefs of our fathers?" asked the troubled minority leader.

"Do as your fathers have done! Again it is spring, and all things must grow and change." Hadar continued, "Your responsibility is great. And having eyes to see, see the revelation all around you! What you are experiencing is neither determined nor random, but creative. You must see or perish!"

After what seemed a long silence in the quiet room, a worried and overwhelmed aid asked, "How could we even begin?"

As Hadar stood to leave, he turned, and raising his walking stick and extending his arms, he was heard, "Begin like this:

In the beginning were the Stars.
And the Earth was born of the Stars.
And all creatures were born of the Earth.
And all peoples became the joy and tears of the Earth.
As she guarded them in the womb of the Sacred Universe.
And it was good . . . "

As Hadar walked to leave the assembly room, he found himself face-to-face with a leader who whispered, "How can you leave us now?" "Because my work is over. I have given you what you need, you only need to want what I have given." And with that, Hadar embraced the man and left.

## CHAPTER FIVE
# THE DEPARTURE

By now, the townspeople had gathered and were hearing the applause from inside the assembly. This raised the people's hopes for peace. Unexplainable warmth and happiness moved through the crowd. As Hadar descended the steps again, a grateful applause from the people began.

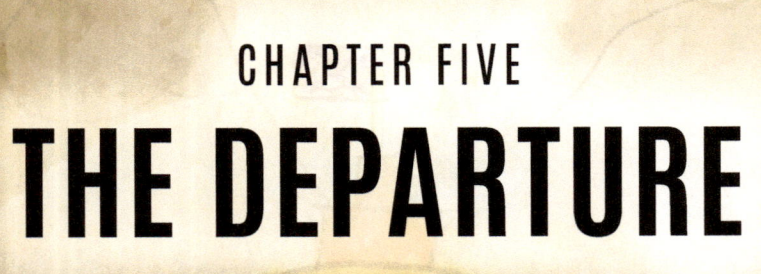

As Hadar walked through the crowd, fewer and fewer people recognized him as he blended into the excitement around him. His work was done. He was no longer needed. He was now again one of the people and anxious to return to his home beyond the border.

A man from the countryside recognized him as he was leaving the capital and called, "Where are you going?" "To the mountains beneath the stars beyond the border." "Will you be alone there in the mountains?" "No, I will be where I can see the stars and care for a great multitude of life that rejoice in me."

As the distance between them grew, the townsman stood watching, now joined by others, who began to understand his vision. As the light from the setting sun focused on Hadar, his robes glowed with all the colors of nature.

Someone asked, "Will he return?"

"He did not say, but I know he is as we want to be, and he will, as he has when there is want or need."

## The End

www.ingramcontent.com/pod-product-compliance
Lightning Source LLC
Chambersburg PA
CBHW041100070526
44579CB00002B/27